Surprise!

SALLY NOLL

Greenwillow Books, New York

For Libby

Gouache paints were used for the full-color art.
The text type is Kabel Medium.

Copyright © 1997 by Sally Noll
All rights reserved. No part of this book may
be reproduced or utilized in any form or by
any means, electronic or mechanical, including
photocopying, recording, or by any information
storage and retrieval system, without permission
in writing from the Publisher, Greenwillow Books,
a division of William Morrow & Company, Inc.,
1350 Avenue of the Americas, New York, NY 10019.
Printed in Hong Kong by South China Printing
Company (1988) Ltd.
First Edition 10 9 8 7 6 5 4 3 2 1

Library of Congress Cataloging-in-Publication Data
Noll, Sally.
Surprise! / by Sally Noll.
    p.   cm.
Summary: Verses featuring the numbers from
one to ten describe a young girl's surprise
when she opens her birthday present.
ISBN 0-688-15170-1 (trade).
ISBN 0-688-15171-X (lib. bdg.)
[1. Cats—Fiction.   2. Birthdays—Fiction.
3. Counting.   4. Stories in rhyme.]   I. Title.
PZ8.3.N736Su   1997   96-36979   CIP   AC

One small Rose

hears
"Surprise, surprise!"

Two little hands
cover her eyes.

Three smiling faces look on from the side.

Four shiny ribbons
get untied.

Five tiny toes
kick and dangle.

Seven
bright
colors,
and still
no clue...

until **eight**
furry stripes
come
peeking
through.

Nine eager eyes keep them in sight.

Then ten happy fingers
wave with delight

at one small kitten
with a soft, wet nose.
One small kitten
for one small Rose.